GW01605618

Beanstalk Books

Series Editor: Alan Blackwood

SBN: 72381123 7
Printed in Great Britain by W. S. Cowell, Ipswich

WE WANT A WHEEL

Written by

Alan Blackwood

Illustrated by

Christine Skilton

NELSON
YOUNG WORLD

We had a cart with big wheels.

It had four big wheels.

One day our cart hit a stone.

A wheel came off.

The cart wouldn't go.

The wheel was broken
all to bits.
We had to find another.

My Dad had an old wheelbarrow.

But that wheel was too big.

Jim's brother had an old motorbike.

But its wheels were too big.

Sally's sister had some old roller-skates.

But those wheels were too small.

We asked Bill's Gran for a wheel off her wheel chair. But she wouldn't give us a wheel.

Then Ann remembered the junk yard.

Perhaps we could find a wheel in the junk yard.

We looked around the junk yard.

There were wheels and wheels.

There were wheels everywhere.

There was lots of old junk. There was an old pram in a corner. It had four wheels as good as new.

We asked the man if we could

have the wheels off the old pram.

6
6

The man said we could.

Look at our cart now!